5758
(7)

D0348060

Life

Paul Cézanne was born at Aix-en-Provence on 19 January 1839, at the end of the decade in which all the other impressionists were born: Pissarro, Manet, Degas, Sisley, Monet and Renoir. His father, Louis-Auguste Cézanne, was not a native of Aix, but had gone there at the age of thirty, about the year 1825, and had taken part in one of the local industries, hat-making. Biographers add that although the Cézanne family were of French origin, they came from Cesana, a village on the Italian slopes of Mont-Genèvre or Monginevro, above Sestriere. A young worker in the Cézanne hat factory, Anne-Elisabeth-Honorine Aubert, became Paul's mother and was married to Louis-Auguste five years later, when her second child, Marie, was aged three; another girl, Rose, was born ten years after the wedding. Louis-Auguste Cézanne was an active and enterprising man, and in spite of the distrust felt by the population of Aix for anyone who was a 'foreigner', he managed to make his way and become successful. In 1847 his sound business acumen led him to buy up the Banque Barges which had become insolvent, and the next year with a partner he founded the banking firm of Cézanne et Cabassol. So began a new period for the Cézanne family, an era of greater prosperity and standing. It was perhaps for reasons of prestige that in 1859 Paul's father bought the property of Jas de Bouffan, a mile or so west of Aix and at one time the residence of the Governor of Provence. The property consisted of thirty-seven acres of land enclosed by a wall, with a magnificent garden of ancient trees and a fine eighteenth-century villa. It was in this villa that the Cézanne family spent their summers, and here Paul learned to understand and communicate with nature. The Jas de Bouffan property was later to play a vital part in the artist's life; nowhere else was he able to work more consistently or more frequently.

Paul had now reached the age of twenty, and what had been just an inclination towards painting was about to become a definite vocation, although there were still many doubts and discouragements to be overcome. Meanwhile, he had already met Emile Zola and Baptiste Baille; this meeting proved a decisive event in his life. At Aix they were called 'the three inseparables'. They met in 1852 at the Collège Bourbon and became firm friends, and the depth of their friendship is revealed in the eloquent exchange of letters which lasted through their years of maturity. Cézanne was a hard-working and serious pupil with a special interest in the ancient languages (it is said that he could write a hundred Latin verses in the course of a morning). He also gained excellent marks in mathematics, history and literature, and was awarded special prizes in all these subjects. The one subject in which he did not excel was drawing; the prizes in drawing were won every year by Emile Zola, the future creator of the naturalist novel. School was not the only activity shared by the three friends. They spent their holidays together in the countryside around Aix, fishing, swimming, reading poetry and playing serenades under a girl's window: Zola played the trumpet, Cézanne the clarinet. They wrote as well: dramas, comedies, poems. For some time still Cézanne continued to fill pages with his verse, and some critics have attempted to trace in these pages the signs of what he later became, that is, the greatest landscape artist of modern painting:

. . . But the yellowed leaves
At the breath of winter have lost
Their freshness, faded are the plants and grasses on
[the banks
Of the stream, while the tree, broken by the fury
[of the winds,
Waves, like an immense skeleton, its bare branches
[in the air.

It is difficult to draw a conclusion, although it is certainly true that the landscape of his native Provence was becoming implanted in Cézanne's heart and mind during those summers.

These then were years of experiment and questioning. Decisions were reached slowly, but for Cézanne painting, was already a part of his innermost being, like a plant growing a little stronger each day. In 1856 he began to attend Professor Gibert's drawing classes at the Aix Art School. Two years later he was awarded a second prize. Looking at some of the works produced at this time, we find it impossible to prophesy Cézanne's future greatness, and above all impossible to foresee that he was to become a great innovator. His drawings at this time were academic, of a cold and scholarly perfection, with a precise and meticulous rendering of anatomy. Here was no indication of those sublime ' hesitations ', those subtle ' anomalies ', which less than twenty years later were to become an unmistakable mark of Cézanne's art. Yet he already had within him that gift of persistence, through all doubts and anxieties, which none of his biographers have failed to point out. Zola was the first to remark on these aspects of Cézanne's character, when in a letter addressed to Baille he asked him to overlook Cézanne's moodiness, his sudden angers and equally sudden depressions: ' Even when you are hurt, you should not be angry with him, but with the evil demon which overcasts his mind. His is a heart of gold, he is a friend who can understand us, mad like us and a dreamer as we are. '

This letter was written in May 1860 from Paris, where Zola had been living since February 1858. The last thing he and Cézanne had done together before his departure was to paint a screen with decorative patterns and ornamental trees. Their separation increased Cézanne's natural unrest: ' Ever since you left,' he wrote, ' I am tormented by grief. This is the truth. You would not recognize me. I feel heavy, stupid and slow.' The year when his father bought the Jas de Bouffan, 1859, was also the year of Cézanne's *baccalauréat*. The decision to devote himself entirely to painting and to leave with Baille to join Zola in Paris became more and more firmly rooted at the conclusion of his high-school studies, but his father saw matters in a different light. With solid common sense he wrote to his son: ' Think of the future: with genius you die, with money you eat. ' But Paul had the support of his mother and sister Marie. To please his father he began to study law, but continued at the same time to plan his journey to the capital. From Paris, Zola sent him a time-table for each day: 'From six till eleven in the morning, you will go to a studio and paint from the nude; then eat; then from twelve to four you will copy old masters in the Louvre and Luxembourg. This will make nine hours' work.' At last, Paul's father gave in. But between the first decision to leave and the actual departure came one of Cézanne's frequent periods of discouragement. He felt trapped in a kind of apathy, born of lack of confidence. He did not react even to Zola's hortatory and encouraging letters: 'If you remain silent, how do you expect to go forward and achieve anything? It is materially impossible. And remember it's not the man who shouts loudest who is right. Speak, if you like, wisely and gently; but by the horns, by the feet, by the tail and navel of the devil, speak!' Slowly and gradually, Cézanne's courage returned and towards the end of April 1861 Louis-Auguste himself accompanied his son to Paris.

No sooner did Paul arrive than he set to work enthusiastically; in fact, he could hardly find the time to be together with Zola. He attended the Académie Suisse, where he met and became a friend of Guillaumin and Pissarro. But most of his time was spent in the Louvre. Cézanne did not feel happy in Paris, with its bustle and confusion. The works of the great masters (Delacroix and Courbet as well as Caravaggio, Rembrandt, Velázquez and Rubens) moved him profoundly, but Paris itself was strange to him, as was the artistic life of the capital. However, he benefited greatly from this first visit. This was the year when the students rose in revolt against the Academy and asked Courbet if he would himself set up a free school of art. As we know, Courbet answered in a famous letter: 'It is the duty of the human spirit to work always on the new, always in the present, starting from acquired results. One should never begin anew, but proceed from synthesis to synthesis, from conclusion to conclusion. Real artists are those who take up an epoch just at the point to which it has been brought by the preceding periods. Going back is the same as doing nothing, it is a pure waste of time . . . Beauty is in nature and is met in reality under the most varied forms. As soon as it has been discovered there, beauty belongs to art, or rather to the artist who knows how to see it . . . Beauty, like truth, is linked to the time in which one lives and to the individual who is capable of perceiving it. ' These ideas were in the air, and were imbuing new life into the stale academic tradition. How then could Cézanne fail to be stirred by these exciting new currents? However, by the end of the year, he was back at Aix: between the desire to act, to succeed, to achieve his ambition as an artist, and his inability to adapt to a new environment and way of life, it was the latter which prevailed.

So he began to work in his father's bank, a resentful and sullen employee. But with each day that passed his urge to return to painting grew stronger. The point came when he could no longer bear to be confined within the walls of the office. It was then that he wrote in an account book the famous couplet:

> *Cézanne, le banquier, ne voit pas sans frémir*
> *Derrière son comptoir naître un peintre à venir.*
> ' Cézanne the banker sees not without trembling
> Behind his counter a future painter being born. '

In November 1862 Cézanne was back in Paris, and he remained there until July 1864. When it was clear that there was absolutely no chance that his decision to become a painter would be reversed, his father said that he should at least set about his career seriously, and sit for the entrance examinations of the Ecole des Beaux-Arts. He did so, but did not pass. His drawings were no longer academic; his hand moved more freely, and an unusual depth of emotion was already present, although still in an uncertain and confused form. What is undeniable, however, is that what Cézanne was now doing, or trying to do, could scarcely be pleasing to the professors of the Ecole des Beaux-Arts. Cézanne himself was not really very concerned about what they might think. He was moving towards a highly romantic kind of painting, in which his sympathies for Delacroix, Daumier and Courbet were apparent. But in Paris he was also enlarging the circle of his acquaintances through his renewed friendship with Guillaumin and Pissarro: this brought him into contact with Bazille, Monet, Sisley and

Renoir. In 1863 in company with Zola he visited the Salon des Refusés, where Manet was showing *Luncheon on the Grass,* the masterpiece whose boldness and originality were found so shocking by the public. He did not meet Manet himself, however, until 1866. *Luncheon on the Grass* exercised a special fascination upon Cézanne, and he considered that the painting advanced and developed the lesson of Courbet in a bolder, fresher and more spontaneous technique. These impressions were all stored up by him, even though, as was always the case, the fruit of his discoveries did not appear until after a long process of maturation.

Cézanne's doubts and periods of unrest were by no means over. In 1864 when he returned to Aix, he was again in a distressed and irritable state. He realised by this time that he needed both Paris and Provence, so in the years 1864-70 he divided his time between the capital and his native countryside.

In 1866 he sent two works to the Salon, as he had done two years before. On the first occasion he did not complain when he was rejected, but this time he protested in a letter to Count Nieuwerkerke, the Director of the Beaux-Arts: 'I cannot accept the unlawful judgment of colleagues whom I have not authorized to judge me. I am therefore writing to you for your support. I wish to appeal to the public and have my work shown in spite of everything . . . Let the Salon des Refusés be re-established; even if I were to be the only one there, I ardently hope the public will know that I do not care to be confused with the gentlemen of the Jury, as they themselves do not wish to have anything to do with me.' This letter expressed an opinion which was shared by many other artists, but Count Nieuwerkerke was certainly not the right person to take up the cudgels on behalf of artists who were innovators. What the Count thought about artists with realist tendencies or whose subject-matter had any connection with the 'present' had already been expressed by him a few years earlier with regard to Millet and Courbet: 'It is the painting of democrats, people who do not change their shirts and want to get the upper hand over decent society; it is an art I do not like; in fact, it disgusts me.'

To make up for this, Cézanne had the consolation of Manet's admiration for his still-lifes. Another source of consolation had been an article by Marius Roux, which had appeared in the local paper *Mémorial d'Aix* in December 1865 on the occasion of the publication of Zola's *La Confession de Claude,* which the author dedicated to his faithful friends Baille and Cézanne. This was the first time mention of Cézanne had been made in the press: ' Cézanne ', wrote Roux, ' has left among us the impression of an intrepid worker and a conscientious pupil. I am waiting for his work to be recognized and on that day I will not be the only one to talk about him. He belongs to a school which has the privilege of provoking criticism. ' Meanwhile, as well as the still-lifes, Cézanne was painting a series of portraits: the Negro Scipion (*pl. 5*), his uncle Dominique, the art critic Valabrègue, the painter Emperaire (*pl. 4*) and his father reading the paper *L'Avènement* in which Zola's ' pieces ' in support of Manet had appeared.

At this time grave events were about to take place in France. The Franco-Prussian War broke out in July; this led to the fall of Napoleon III, the proclamation of the Third Republic, the armistice of January 1871, and then the insurrection which set up in the capital the first people's government in modern history, the Commune. When on 5 April Courbet made his appeal to the artists of Paris, which was surrounded by Prussian soldiers, the great amphitheatre of the Faculty of Medicine was filled to overflowing with painters and sculptors, and the names of the members who were elected to the Committee of the Artists' Federation included those of the greatest French artists of the time: Corot, Courbet, Daumier, Manet. The support given by the artist-craftsmen to the Commune was so prompt and effective that their forces alone made up an entire company of combatants. Soon afterwards, in a week of repression, ' the week of blood ', as it was called, the troops of Thiers put down all popular resistance. Courbet was arrested, tried and exiled.

All these events seem to have left Cézanne unmoved, for all his thoughts and attention centred upon his work, now daily becoming more masterly and individual. During the war he took refuge at L'Estaque, near Marseilles. He took with him Hortense Fiquet, the young model he had met in Paris in 1869. Their son was born in 1872, and they were married in 1886. This was a fruitful time for Cézanne, the beginning of the great period of his art. We need only mention some of the works produced then to appreciate this: *The Black Clock* (*pl. 8*), *View of L'Estaque, Street in Pontoise*, 1872, *House and Tree, Old Path at Auvers, The house of Dr Gachet at Auvers*, 1873 (*pl. 16*). As the last two titles indicate, Cézanne had moved from L'Estaque to Auvers, and was staying in the house of that same doctor, an amateur painter and friend of artists, who seventeen years later was to give shelter to Van Gogh, exactly one year before the artist's death. At Auvers Cézanne also painted *The Suicide's House* (*pl. 13*), one of his first masterpieces. This work affirmed his position in the impressionist movement. The group of new painters joined together in 1874 for their first exhibition. Present were: Sisley, Renoir, Pissarro, Degas, Monet, Berthe Morisot, Guillaumin, and several lesser-known artists. Monet showed the famous painting which gave its name to the whole movement: *Impression, rising sun*. Cézanne exhibited *The Suicide's House* and also a painting quite opposite in inspiration: *A modern Olympia* (*pl. 15*). This work was based on Manet's famous painting and was still romantic in style, though the colours had become more luminous and bright. Manet himself did not exhibit, perhaps thinking he could still aspire to official acclaim. The main purpose of the exhibition, which was organized at the Galerie Nadar in the Boulevard des Capucines, was to oppose the tyranny of the Salon. It therefore had a definite bias towards expressions of revolt against the traditional artistic structures. It also, of course, aimed to affirm the values of a new vision of art.

Public and critics alike received the exhibition with a chorus of protest and scorn. Cézanne's works received the worst treatment. It was probably partly because of the treatment he received at his time that he was later always reluctant to send in to exhibitions. Of the eight exhibitions of impressionist paintings which took place from 1876 to 1886 Cézanne took part in only one. This was the third exhibition, in 1877, where he showed seventeen canvases, painted at L'Estaque, Pontoise and Auvers. Their reception was no different, however: the same malevolence on the part of the public, the same hostility from the critics. Yet Cézanne's work was proceeding with ever greater purpose and conviction; true, his doubts did not leave him, but by his impassioned and obdurate persistence he succeeded in overcoming them.

In those years he painted, among others, such works as *The Hermitage at Pontoise, The Sideboard, Madame Cézanne in a Red Armchair, The Pond at Jas de Bouffan* and *Portrait of Chocquet*. Some of these paintings already show signs of a trend towards a more structural form of impressionism. Around 1878 there thus began what has been called Cézanne's period of constructive analysis. Typical works of the period are *L'Estaque, seen over the Bay of Marseilles, Winding street, Tablecloth and Fruit Dish, House by Mont Sainte-Victoire, Still-life with apples* (*pls 24-5*). Cézanne was in Paris at this time, and met Huysmans at Zola's house. In 1882 he was at last accepted by the Salon, for in spite of rejections he had been sending in regularly, and never failed to do so, if for no other reason than to show his father that he was a serious painter, a ' professional '. His acceptance this time, however, was on the grounds that he was a ' pupil of Guillemet ', and this was the first and last time that he was ever accepted by the Salon.

In the years which followed, Cézanne strove for an ever greater definition of the constituent elements of the image, and around 1890 this became the so-called ' syntheticism ' of Cézanne. He stayed in Paris, Médan, Pontoise, Aix, L'Estaque and Gardanne, always immersed in his painting to the exclusion of all else. He was seen with Zola, with Pissarro, Renoir and Monet, and also met Monticelli. On his father's death in 1886 he inherited a solid fortune. But grief at his father's death was accompanied by another cruel blow. This came to him from the dear friend of his youth, and it caused Cézanne a sorrow which could never be healed. Although he spoke of it to no one, it could be seen that the grief was bitter and irremediable. For it was in this year that Zola published *L'Oeuvre*, his novel of the life of a painter, Claude Lantier. The character of

Lantier had more than one point of resemblance with Cézanne, although in certain other facets it resembled Manet. While he realized that Zola had created a literary character in which the imagination of the author played a large part, Cézanne recognized himself substantially in this portrait, and Zola's judgment wounded him bitterly. Lantier was a painter who hanged himself from a beam in his studio in front of the work which he was impotent to complete. The tone of Zola's story is tragic, and there is never any hint of disparagement. But perhaps it was partly because of the sincere compassion expressed in the novel that Cézanne's grief was so inconsolable.

Zola had in fact moved away from his impressionist friends and had ended by no longer believing in them, after having been their most valiant champion and defender. *L'Oeuvre* was only a milder statement of the view he was to express a few years later, when he explicitly stated his regret at having fought ' on behalf of those spots, those reflections, that breaking-up of light ' in which, he said, the strength of the impressionists' original emotion in the face of nature had become exhausted. On 4 April of that year, Cézanne wrote the following letter to Zola: ' I have just received *L'Oeuvre* which you were good enough to send me. I thank the author of the *Rougon Macquart* novels for this gesture of affection and ask him to let me clasp his hand, in remembrance of the past. With all the enthusiasm of the old times, your Cézanne. ' This then, ' the past ', ' the old times ', was all that remained of their friendship; as far as the present was concerned, after *L'Oeuvre,* their friendship was over for good. No more letters passed between them, there were no more greetings and they did not meet again.

' Isolation, that's what I deserve ', so Cézanne confessed to Claude Bernard, the young painter and writer who was a friend of Van Gogh. But though he clung to this choice, and his irritability increased still more as a result of diabetes, he was becoming the centre of a group of admirers, young artists and writers: Gustave Geffroy, Joachim Gasquet, Maurice Denis. In 1901, Denis exhibited at the Salon of the Société nationale des Beaux-Arts a large canvas entitled *Homage to Cézanne.* A still-life by the solitary of Aix appeared in the centre, and a group of artists were arranged around it: Odilon Redon, Vuillard, Sérusier, Bonnard, and Denis himself. Among the artists, however, a new figure now made his appearance. This was Ambroise Vollard, the most active and enlightened dealer in modern art between the years 1890 and 1910. It was Vollard who took an active interest in Cézanne's work and organized his first large exhibition in 1895. Although once again this exhibition did not persuade the public to accept Cézanne, yet it did bring him some esteem among certain *avant-garde* collectors and a wider circle of art-lovers. His painting had now reached the furthest stage in its development. After a journey to Switzerland in 1891, he spent some time at Fontainebleau. The year 1892 had produced some outstanding successes in his painting. The process of structural synthesis to which all his efforts were tending in that year attained what was possibly its highest culmination in the five versions of *The Card Players* (*pls 50-1*). In the year before the Vollard exhibition he had spent some time at Giverny, where Monet too was staying. Through him Cézanne became acquainted with Georges Clémenceau, Octave Mirbeau and Geffroy.

But as a result of one of the fits of temper which were becoming more and more frequent, Cézanne set off again suddenly from Giverny for Aix, leaving all his paintings at the hotel: it was Monet who had them crated and sent to him. ' Here I am buried again in the South – which I should never have left – about to rush off in pursuit of the chimera of art. ' Thus he wrote to Monet from his refuge at Aix. He found his mother in ill-health. Cézanne was sincerely devoted to his mother and for the three years remaining to her he surrounded her with every care and attention, dividing his time between painting and his mother's bedside. When she died, in October 1898, he had to agree for legal reasons connected with her estate to sell the Jas de Bouffan. To his grief at the death of his mother there was therefore added the further loss of the places and the house where he had spent so much of his life. He then moved into a house in the Rue Boulegon in Aix; he had already found a cottage above the Aix dam where he could paint, even sleep at times, and keep his canvases. He liked this place and would gladly have bought it, but the owner was not willing to sell.

In 1899 Cézanne sent three works to the Salon des Indépendants, an organization founded in 1884 so that artists could make their works known without having to submit them to a jury. He showed there again three years later. He was persuaded to exhibit his works by his new young friends, who considered him a master. But surprising things were happening: the Nationalgalerie in Berlin bought one of his landscapes, and the name Cézanne crossed a frontier. This seems, at least in part, to have compensated Cézanne for his many disappointments. He now bought some land on the road to Lauves, north of Aix, and had a spacious studio built there. His tenacious passion for work continued to sustain and at the same time torment him.

In spite of the break in their friendship, when Zola died in 1902 Cézanne felt great sorrow. But it was Zola's death which, almost by chance, showed how Cézanne's fame had now grown. When Zola's collection was put up for sale in March of the following year, ten youthful works by Cézanne fetched a far higher price than the work of the other impressionists, as much as 3,000 or 4,000 francs as compared with 2,000 for a Monet and 900 or 500 for a Pissarro. This was the preparation for the triumph of the Salon d'Automne, a newly-founded association in which the artist members themselves acted as jury. Cézanne was given a room to himself, and was acclaimed at long last. Jules Renard wrote in his diary on 21 October 1904: ' At the Salon d'Automne . . . Cézanne, the barbarian. Many famous daubs have had to be admired before liking this carpenter of colour '. His long struggle and fidelity to art were at last rewarded. In the following year he sent another nine works to the Salon d'Automne and in the same year also exhibited in the Salon des Indépendants. His former diffidence seems to have left him. Meanwhile he did not cease working intensively. After seven years of studies, sketches and experiments he completed *The Great Bathers*, now in Philadelphia (*pls 70-1*).

On 15 October 1906, Cézanne was painting outside when a heavy storm blew up and he caught cold. Yet he continued to think about his unfinished paintings, and two days later he wrote a stiff note to his paint-dealer: 'Eight days ago I ordered from you ten tubes of burnt lake no. 7. I have not yet heard from you. What has happened? Answer me, and quickly, please.' On 20 October, his sister Marie summed up the situation dramatically in a letter to Paul, the artist's son, who was in Paris with his mother: 'Your father caught a chill on Monday... He stayed out a few hours in the rain, they brought him home on a laundry cart and two men had to put him to bed. The next morning he went out to the garden early to work on a portrait of Vallier, under the lime-tree: he came away dying.' Cézanne died on 22 October; his wife and son rushed to Aix but were too late to see him alive. He was sixty-seven. On the first anniversary of his death, the artists of the Salon d'Automne put on a retrospective exhibition of fifty-five of his canvases and a large number of watercolours.

Thus began the posthumous fame of Cézanne. In a survey by the *Mercure de France* in 1905, the question was asked: 'What do you think of Cézanne?' Paul Sérusier replied: 'If a tradition is born out of our epoch – and I dare to hope that it will be – it is from Cézanne that it will be born.' With the 1907 exhibition in the Salon d'Automne the 'tradition' of Cézanne was a reality.

Works

The various *avant-garde* movements of contemporary art arose out of a confrontation with impressionism. Its basic concept, freedom, was accepted by them all, but it seemed that impressionism had stopped short at an external and superficial recording of reality. Rejoicing at the advent of expressionism, Hermann Bahr wrote in 1916: 'The impressionist is man reduced to a gramophone of the external world.' But already eight years earlier, when writing of Braque, Guillaume Apollinaire had spoken of impressionism as 'a period of ignorance and frenzy'. Picasso too, on visiting an exhibition of impressionist works at about this time, is said to have looked at the paintings and then exclaimed: 'Here we can see that it is raining, we can see the sun is shining, but nowhere can we see painting.' Yet it was just at this time that admiration for Cézanne by the most advanced artists, especially the cubists, had become an established and concrete fact. It was about then that Léger wrote: ' I wonder what present-day painting would have become without Cézanne. For a long time I have worked with his painting. I could not succeed in breaking away from it, or cease exploring and discovering it. Cézanne taught me the love of forms and volumes and made me concentrate on drawing. I realized then that his drawing must be rigid and in no way sentimental. ' These words already contain a statement of many of the reasons why, although Cézanne belonged to the generation of the impressionists, he was not included in the negative judgment passed on them by the new generation of artistic innovators.

The cubists blamed the impressionists for their lack of rigour and stylistic coherence, and especially for the episodic character of their painting. It is clear that these reproaches spring from the situation of opposition and revolt out of which the *avant-garde* arose, yet it is also true that the theories of impressionism easily lent themselves to a criticism of this kind. Besides, was not Gauguin the first to begin when he said: ' The impressionists look all round, with the eye, and not at the centre, with the mind '? With slow determination, Cézanne had put to himself the problem of how to overcome the ' fleeting ' aspect of impressionism by a painting of solidity and definition. Light, which in impressionist painting vibrated and darted over every object, merging into one palpitating brilliance, in Cézanne was absorbed by objects and itself became form, in unison with colour. Cézanne rejected the ' impression ' in favour of a deeper comprehension of reality. At the very time when all the generally accepted values of the nineteenth century were being re-examined, and what had seemed to be incontrovertible truths were again called in question, Cézanne strove to construct something firm and lasting, something which would resist fragmentation. The broad canvas of history and emotion, against which Cézanne's greatly admired Delacroix, Daumier and Courbet had moved, had now shrunk, as the artist became an ever more solitary figure. A full awareness of the artist's changed and difficult condition is shown in Van Gogh's belief that artists no longer formed part of society, but were 'opposed' to it, 'rejected' in the same way as society rejected the prostitute, 'our friend and sister'. Cézanne certainly did not yet possess a similar awareness, but neither can his solitude be explained merely by his difficult temperament. His position did not, in fact, differ greatly from Van Gogh's, though whereas liberation of emotion was all-important in Van Gogh, in Cézanne the emotions were suppressed and constricted within a formal structure.

It was Picasso who saw the profound connection binding Cézanne and Van Gogh to the same harsh destiny: 'Cézanne would never have interested me,' he told Zervos, 'if he had thought and lived like Jacques-Emile Blanche, even if the apple he painted had been ten times more beautiful. What interests me is the anxiety of Cézanne, the torment of Van Gogh, that is, the drama of man. The rest is unimportant.' Picasso has realized that Cézanne and Van Gogh are the two faces of the same historical situation. Cézanne's research into a blocked form was therefore not undertaken purely for aesthetic reasons, but was also a way of creating something durable and of reaching some kind of certainty. The Provençal landscapes which Cézanne and Van Gogh painted in the same period provide striking evidence of the difference between them, and this contrast is the more apparent as the backgrounds were so very similar: for Van Gogh, landscape provides a stage upon which his violent emotions are enacted, so that it too becomes violent and convulsed; while for Cézanne the same landscape is a solid reality which he wishes to preserve in an equally solid form, conceived as the only possible antidote to his inner unrest.

From this point of view there is really something heroic about Cézanne's technique, for in him too there lived romantic impulses, he too felt the power of Delacroix and Daumier, of El Greco and Tintoretto, but he forced himself to follow the path of Courbet and Poussin, though without, of course, rejecting any of the discoveries of impressionism. No one, I think, has pointed out this 'truth' of Cézanne better than Jacques Rivière. Writing only four years before his death, he said, 'Cézanne was not the fumbling artist of genius a certain legend has tended to show. On the contrary, his watercolours are so amazingly skilful that they are equalled only by the virtuosity of the Japanese; on the white sheet of paper the whole structure of a landscape is uncovered by a few touches of colour, which are so exactly right that they make the intervening spaces speak and yield up their innermost meaning. Yet Cézanne always holds himself back, fearing to substitute his own personality for its sincerity; he imposes on his brush a faithful slowness. Application dominates him like a passion; he bends his head devotedly, keeps silent the better to see; imprisons the form he is copying within the circle of his attention; and, since it moves, he never breathes easily until he has captured it. Time and again his brush wishes to abandon itself to its own volition, but he holds it back, forces it to remain ' ruthless '. So, if we think we can see hesitations in his painting, these are not the outcome of the impotence of a hand too heavy or too unskilful to follow precisely the outline of objects, but are only the scruples of an unremit- ting patience, intent on moderating the outbursts of his too eager skill. '

The problem of completed form thus remains the essential problem of Cézanne, but it is to be interpreted in the light of the completeness of his aspirations. The ideal of Cézanne is an ideal of classicism, stated at the outset of a completely anti-classical period.

While accepting the ' naturalism ' of the impressionists, Cézanne wished to eliminate its more ephemeral aspects and restore to painting the restraint and measure of the masters of classicism: ' Imagine Poussin completely done over again from nature and you will have a classic as I understand it. ' As he liked to say, Cézanne wanted to make out of impressionism something ' lasting, like the art of the museums '. His was not an academic dream, but a spiritual necessity: ' Everything we see, surely, melts away? Nature is always the same, but nothing of it endures, so far as we can see. Our art must give a sense of its duration, must make us feel that it is eternal. What lies behind the natural phenomenon? Perhaps nothing; perhaps everything. Therefore my hands perform their task, taking from right and left, here and there, everywhere, its colours, its tones; I fix them, place them side by side, and they form lines, "become" objects, rocks, trees, without my thinking about it. They assume volume. My canvas ... does not vacillate, it is true, compact, complete.'

Like all the other impressionists, Cézanne inherited from Courbet a hatred for fantasy and the literary element in art. A painting, in his view, must live by the strength of paint alone, must rely only on the means which are proper to it, without the aid of melodrama or anecdote. For him as for Courbet, however, this does not mean giving up the rendering of a sense of the real, by virtue of painting. 'My method,' he said, 'is hatred for the fantastic image, it is realism, but a realism, let it be understood, which is full of greatness, the heroism of the real.' This attitude of Cézanne towards reality is what made so much impressionist art appear frivolous in the eyes of the cubists when they came to compare it with his.

This was no longer, of course, the great period of realism. The most vigorous ideological positions of the nineteenth century were losing their foothold and crumbling, but at his provincial retreat in Provence, Cézanne entrenched himself immovably within a single circumscribed problem, that of form as an absolute totality of representation. From that position, he resisted, conducted his battle, and at the same time opened up new directions to modern art, just as Van Gogh had done in another way. In a recent period when formal values were praised exclusively, Cézanne has even been interpreted as a purely abstract painter; but even if his experimentation in formal values, taken alone, might have made such an interpretation possible, the whole of Cézanne's experience has been of far greater richness and complexity.

Cézanne's creative process cannot really be reduced either to a scientific attitude which developed the optical discoveries of impressionism to the extent of splitting up objects, or to a simple plane of abstraction. For Cézanne abstraction begins after he has gained a deep insight into his subject, and even at this point it is never a one-sided process. Cézanne studied nature minutely and wished to learn all its secrets. 'To paint a landscape well, I must first discover all its geological features.' This was not meant to be a witty remark: to testify to the contrary, there are the Sunday walks Cézanne took with a childhood friend, Professor Marion, whom he questioned on the physical history of the earth and the structure of the Aix countryside. When therefore, Cézanne speaks of the 'truth' of the real world, he means something precise. He does not aim to do a generic landscape painting, but a painting in which 'the perfume of the pines, which is sharp in the sun, must be wedded to the green scent of the meadows, the odour of the stones, the perfume of the distant marble of the Mont Sainte-Victoire...' This, he continues, is 'what must be rendered, and only with colours, without literature'.

Colour is the only specific medium of the painter. The artist has only this medium through which to achieve the miracle of art. But is colour not also nature's basic way of showing itself? Once, 'a landscape used to be composed in the same way as a historical scene, from the outside; it was not realized that nature is more in depth than on the surface. One can modify, decorate and dress up the surface, but one cannot attain depth without attaining truth. Colours are the expression of this truth at the surface, they rise up from the roots of the world.' Then, just as nature manifests its truth through coloured forms, so too must the painting, through its coloured forms, manifest the poetic substance on which it feeds. This is the conception of Cézanne. As we see, the so-called 'positivistic naturalism' of the impressionists has moved up on to another plane, becoming a sort of terrestrial or cosmic immanence where man is both an integral part and a consciousness.

The work of art is thus the outcome of knowledge and emotion at one and the same time, organized by the artist into the image. The objectivity of the impressionists, the essential purpose of which was the pure registration of impressions, is now abandoned. In Cézanne there is meditation and reflection: 'Landscape becomes humanized, is reflected and thinks in me.' He is clearly aware of this problem: 'I am the subjective consciousness of this landscape, and my canvas is its objective consciousness. My canvas and the landscape are both outside me, but the latter is chaotic, haphazard, confused, without logical life, without any kind of rational being, while the former is permanent, categorized, and it participates in the world of ideas.'

The modern problem of the autonomy of art had now been stated: the painting is a self-contained entity, with laws which are absolutely its own. On the other hand, this new reality does not deny its connection with its origins, but affirms it. This is because for Cézanne creation is never merely a matter of speculation, as it had already tended to become in certain works by Seurat. Cézanne wants the painting to live through the life which is contained in it, he wants it to be autonomous and to exist only by virtue of its own qualities, without any admixture of literature, music, or even science. But at the same time he knows that the work cannot live unless it has been created by all the powers of the artist in unison with the powers of the natural world: 'Every one of my brushstrokes is like a little of my blood, mixed with a little of my model's blood, in the sun, the light, in colour. We must live in harmony, my model, my colours, and I.'

The way of Cézanne is therefore not the way of abstraction. One might perhaps say that he is an 'organic' painter. Even colour is not an abstract or metaphorical entity to him, but a natural energy in its own right: 'Colour, I would say, is biological, it is alive and it alone can make things live.' Outside symbolism, psychology and abstraction, Cézanne's colour is the very life of the objects which are contained within the rectangle of his canvas. This is perhaps what constitutes Cézanne's own form of classicism.

For the painter colour is therefore also form. This is the meaning of Cézanne's famous equation 'form = colour'. Linear design in itself must not exist, for it does not exist in nature. Line is implicit in the rounded form. The more colour grows and gains in precision and harmony, the more the 'line' of objects will appear, but it must appear through form. The painting of Cézanne cannot therefore be graphic or linear, but is a painting of volumes. His urgent need to 'produce form' resulted in that flat, dry, structural brushstroke which is one of the basic elements of his style, and in the slowness of execution which has become legendary. He was forced to simplify and condense. In one of his most frequently-quoted letters, Cézanne summed up his theory of the simplification of forms in a statement which was later to serve the cubists so well: ' In nature everything is modelled according to three basic shapes: the sphere, the cone, the cylinder. We must learn to paint these shapes, then we shall be able to do whatever we wish. '

But once these shapes were created, they had to be placed in relationship to each other, and this posed the problem of planes, of their inter-relationship and their meeting-points: the problem, in short, of the architecture of the painting. So we come to another essential feature of Cézanne's original treatment of form, and the one, perhaps, which has had the greatest consequences for modern art: the beginnings of a new kind of perspective.

Cézanne's attempt to render the three-dimensional quality of objects in such a way as to give them weight and substance forced him inexorably to look at objects no longer from one point of view, but from several. It was only in this way that he could succeed in showing the planes and volumes most effectively. Within the framework of a painting one single object was represented in various perspectives, being distorted either in a vertical or horizontal direction, and similarly, the line of the horizon was no longer a straight horizontal, but became adapted to the architectural requirements of the painting. Such a way of ' seeing ' meant that an object was viewed from several angles simultaneously and arranged on the canvas in a new way, thus creating proportions and relationships differing from those of the Renaissance tradition. In this connection, a number of interesting observations were made by Maurice Merleau-Ponty in an essay on Cézanne: ' Through its fidelity to natural phenomena, Cézanne's research into perspective laid bare all that recent psychology was later to formulate. The kind of perspective experienced by us, that of our perception, is not a geometric or photographic perspective: in our own perception, nearby objects seem to be smaller, and far-off objects larger, than they appear on a photograph... To say that a circle seen obliquely is seen as an ellipse is to substitute for effective perception the view of what we should see if we were cameras: what we actually see is a form which oscillates around the ellipse without being an ellipse. In a portrait of Madame Cézanne, the hem of the hangings on either side of the figure does not form a straight line; but it is known that if a straight line passes under a wide strip of paper, the two visible sections appear distorted. The table of Gustave Geffroy is placed in the lower part of the painting, but as our eye travels over a wide surface, it picks up images from different viewpoints, and the total surface is curved. It is true that by bringing these distortions to the canvas the artist fixes them and arrests the spontaneous movement by which they are amassed one over the other in perception and tend towards a geometric perspective ... (but) through the genius of Cézanne, perspective distortions cease to be visible in themselves when the painting is looked at as a whole, and, just as in natural vision, they only contribute towards a general impression of an order which is in process of coming into being, an object appearing and coagulating in front of our eyes. '

Cézanne's distortions were therefore as far from being arbitrary as could possibly be-imagined: they were the result, as he said, of the intervention of a 'logic' within the impressionist 'optics'. But it is clear that all Cézanne's achievements in this field came into being and were established only as the result of an incessant fatigue and tension, lasting through to the end of his life. This strain is referred to in a letter written in September 1906, one month before his death: 'My mind is in such a confused state and I am so disturbed that I was afraid, at one moment, that my weak reason would be affected... Now I believe I am better and can think more correctly along the line of my studies. Will I ever attain the end which I have sought and pursued for so long? I continue to study from nature and appear to progress slowly'. In order to understand Cézanne's achievements more fully, one must therefore examine at least the most significant stages of his long journey.

The first time Cézanne's inner preoccupation becomes explicit is between the years 1860-70, when he experimented in various ways. I have indicated which artists specially influenced him at this time. For example, in a painting such as *Orgy*, executed between 1864-8, the influence of Venetian art, especially the painting of Veronese and Tintoretto, is apparent – the colour of Veronese, with its intense blues and reds, and the loose design of Tintoretto; while in a work such as *The Washing of the Dead Man*, painted in 1867-9, there are hints of Caravaggio in the dramatic fall of light and shade on the outstretched body of the corpse and on the two figures intent on their pious task. In other works, such as *The Robbers and the Ass (pls 2-3)* and *Melted Snow at L'Estaque*, painted in 1869-70, the dominant influence appears to be Daumier: strong colours, enclosed within a sombre background, and vigorously defined by dark outlines. Daumier himself had painted the same subject of *The Robbers and the Ass* in a well-known work. In all these works we see that at that time Cézanne's preferences lay in erotic and tragic themes. When the subject did not specifically fall into either of these categories, as in the case of a landscape, then he frequently filled the sky with dark clouds, and spread over the countryside the light of an imminent storm. But in general he chose subjects which were in tune with his romantic and ardent nature, with his restless and passionate spirit, and although such subjects were sometimes literary in their nature and origin, they were always generously lived in the imagination. Some of the titles illustrate this trend: *Sorrow (pl. 1)*, *Rape*, *The Crime*, *The Strangled Woman*. Cézanne's manner of painting was also adapted to this kind of subject: an energetic and rather summary brushstroke, thickly-applied paint. This was a kind of 'ideal' painting, entirely opposed to direct painting from nature. But, as I have said, Cézanne's experiments at this time were many and varied, just as there were numerous influences acting on him, from Delacroix to Courbet. In the end it was the realism of Courbet, amended by contact with Manet, which became the dominant influence on Cézanne's art.

In certain works, Cézanne already revealed the new direction in which he was moving. Among these works are those which deal with subjects Manet had also painted, even to the extent of repeating the same title that Manet had invented, as in *Luncheon on the Grass*, for example. But this new direction was still more obvious in a work such as *Paul Alexis Reading a Manuscript to Zola*, completed about the same date. Here the colour had become softer and the vision more direct, while the energy of Cézanne's brushstroke appeared in the unfinished figure of Zola, painted with a firm and sharply defined touch. The painting which best sums up the experiments of this period of Cézanne's research is *The Black Clock* (*pl. 8*): in this work Cézanne's particular inclination for consistency of form and structural solidity of objects is already taking shape. His colours, however, are still applied thickly and with layers of grey and dark shadows. A freer use of colour began to appear in such works as the landscape in Munich (*pls 6-7*), which like *The Black Clock* may be dated about 1870.

But the change in Cézanne occurred just between that date and the first impressionist exhibition, in 1874. In this respect, Pissarro's influence was decisive. He was still painting works such as *A modern Olympia* (*pls 14-15*) with literary and romantic overtones, although in an ironic vein, but in the same year, 1872, and the following year, he painted *House and Tree* and *The Suicide's House* (*pl. 13*), where a relationship with nature, light and the innermost 'truth of things' outside and beyond any references to literature, became fixed and permanent. His palette changed, and he adopted the bright colour Pissarro urged, the colour of impressionism. However, he was still hesistant over the problem of using colour in divided or superimposed tones, and did not solve this until the years 1874-5. Even at this time, however, the most important works always reveal a difference between colour as used by Cézanne and by the other impressionists, and this difference is easy to detect. It was at this time that Cézanne began to stress the geometric shapes in landscape — something which hardly interested the impressionists at all. If a landscape contained roofs, then he instinctively accentuated their square, rectangular or rhomboid shapes by the use of vibrant but toning colours, with separate blues and reds (*pl. 17*). And this difference can also be observed in the brushstroke: from then on it no longer moved with sharp and rapid touches, but already tended to follow the structure of objects, in a vertical or horizontal movement: it was a more 'applied' brushstroke than before.

But the difference between Cézanne and the other impressionists can be seen even more clearly in the still-lifes and portraits, for example in the portrait of *Madame Cézanne in a red armchair*, probably painted at the end of

1877. If we note specially the face, the jacket and the skirt, we can immediately see the 'method' which Cézanne was working out: in this painting colour was already present in the form of blocks, areas and strips, and was used for the purpose of modelling and shaping the forms. This produced a disciplined yet spacious composition in which every previous excess of temperament was held in check. Monet used to say: 'I should like to paint as a bird sings.' Nothing could be farther from Cézanne at this stage than this profession of spontaneity. For he was now abandoning the ideal of the 'impression' for one of 'sensation', that is, for an impression of a kind which is durable, not fleeting; for a total sensation, in which sense perceptions become one with the virtues of consciousness and mind.

It was this concept, which became strengthened and completely defined around 1878, which led Cézanne into an area of research that was his alone. A more and more intent and patient study of nature characterized these years, when he put his method to the test of fire and proved its validity. In a way one could say that this was Cézanne's 'programmatic' period: when he analysed objects, arranged them in simplified compositions and emphasized their volumes. This period extended at least to the end of 1882. From this date until about 1887, his painting acquired a broader and more ample dimension.

This was the period of the great views of L'Estaque, the Bay of Marseilles, and the first paintings of Mont Sainte-Victoire. When figures were included, however, he did not renounce their stability and monumentality but tended to immerse them in a softer or more atmospheric ambience; this trend continued from the early *Two Bathers* (*pl. 36*) and *Three Bathers* of 1882 to the *Great Bather* of 1887. It seems that at about this date Cézanne wanted to bring together the conclusions of the various earlier phases, and move in the direction of a vigorous synthesis of all the modelled elements. From more than one point of view, this seems to be the most typical of all Cézanne's works. For now, in a number of prodigious masterpieces, the problems of the 'construction' of the image had become perfectly fused with the impressionists' concern with 'natural truth': light, colour and form became vital and took on solidity through an inner cohesion in which all distinctions or priorities were finally abolished. At the summit of this process are the version of *The Card Players* (*pls 50-1*). The French tradition of earthy, peasant painting, from the Le Nain brothers to Courbet, was taken up again in these works with a vigour and purity without compare: the solemnity of the card players strikes no attitudes, but is identified with the basic quality of the gestures, the feeling of man's duration and of his remote roots.

Included in this period of synthesis, which is therefore a synthesis of form and vision together, are such works as: *Woman with coffee pot*, 1890-4 (*pl. 52*), *Boy in a red waistcoat*, 1890-5 (*pl. 58*), *Smoker leaning on his elbow*, 1895-1900, a group of still-lifes, and a series of landscapes which are both airy and solid. But once again these amazing achievements did not mark the end of Cézanne's development. It must also be understood, of course, that his periods of trial and experimentation followed a less rectilinear pattern than might be supposed from the account which is given here in broad outline; indeed, the 'comings and goings' of Cézanne within the course of his development are far more numerous than could appear from a critical description, however accurate. Nevertheless, it is a fact that in this development certain salient moments emerge, and it is these which are given prominence in these pages. Among these salient moments must certainly be included the period comprising the last years of his life, from 1900-6. These were the years dominated by the themes of the Bathers and Mont Sainte-Victoire. An awareness of nature seized him with a poignancy which he had never known before in such sweet and disturbing violence. This was Cézanne's 'grand finale', a lyrical period, with tender skies and soft light, blues and greens, air and fragrance, and a nostalgia for nature as a haven of purity and enchantment. Cézanne's 'constructivism' had not disappeared, but now seemed to act on impulse. The painting, *The Great Bathers*, in Philadelphia Museum, completed in 1905 (*pls 70-1*) may be considered the culmination of this last period of Cézanne's activity. What he had visualized as 'classicism', as the eternal element in sensation and at the same time as a 'natural truth', is found here palpitating with life. Cézanne had achieved the impossible: a form of painting which is 'classical' without classicism, 'romantic' without romanticism, 'impressionistic' without impressionism.

It is difficult to provide a definition which really touches the substance of Cézanne's art. Sérusier has written: 'One says about an apple which is painted by an insensitive artist: "I could eat it". Of an apple by Cézanne, one says: "It is beautiful!" No one would dare to peel it, it is more likely that one would feel like copying it. This is where Cézanne's spirituality lies. And I avoided the word "idealism" deliberately, because the ideal apple is one which whets the appetite, while Cézanne's apple speaks to the spirit through the eyes.' It is perhaps in this judgment that we may find the beginnings of a real understanding of Cézanne: an understanding, that is, of an art wherein the impressions gained by an immediate contact with nature – impressions neither impaired nor falsified by extraneous elements – join indissolubly with the consciousness of the spirit. Is Cézanne's painting, therefore, the result of an 'awareness of the world of sensation', at a moment when every other accepted truth appeared to have become a matter for doubt? Many have sought to show that this is so. The untouched quality of the world and characters of Cézanne thus becomes part of the broader concept of nineteenth-century philosophy, which sought escape in a return to the purity and innocence of primordial nature. This tendency can be traced in the work of many artists, from Gauguin to the expressionists. But in Cézanne there is something which goes beyond escapist theories, for Cézanne is the artist who laid the foundations for a new certitude in modern art. That is why Cézanne, together with Van Gogh, has been such an invigorating force in contemporary art, even though his work has not always been completely understood. One could say more – his has probably been the most active and invigorating of the influences which have determined the course of the art of the twentieth century.

Cézanne and the Critics

Appreciation of Cézanne, as we can see from what has been said above, came slowly and grudgingly. After Zola broke away from him and began to reject his ideas, the first favourable comment on Cézanne's painting is found in the words and writings of younger artists, neo-impressionists and symbolists, and in newspaper articles by one or two especially far-sighted critics. It was not until about 1920 that he gained wider acclaim, when many books were written about him, leading to the standard work by Lionello Venturi, *Cézanne, son art, son œuvre*, 2 volumes, Paris 1936. This is a catalogue which describes 1634 works in chronological order. The present book has been based on this study, apart from a few questions of chronology: all that remains to be said is that the dates are nearly always approximate, because with few exceptions Cézanne did not date or sign his paintings.

To assist the reader, the essential bibliography is divided into three sections:

REMINISCENCES AND LETTERS

Zola, *La confession de Claude*, Paris 1866; *Correspondance*, edited by J. Rewald, Paris 1937; E. Bernard, 'Souvenirs sur P. Cézanne', in *Mercure de France*, Paris October 1907; A. Vollard, *P. Cézanne*, Paris 1914; M. Lafargue, 'Souvenirs sur P. Cézanne', in *L'Amour de l'Art*, Paris January 1921; C. Camoin, 'Souvenirs sur P. Cézanne', in *L'Amour de l'Art*, January 1921; E. Bernard, *Souvenirs sur P. Cézanne*, Paris 1921; L. Larguier, *Le dimanche avec P. Cézanne*, Paris 1925; C. Pissarro, *Lettres à son fils Lucien*, Paris 1950.

MONOGRAPHS AND SPECIAL STUDIES

E. Bernard, 'P. Cézanne', *Les Hommes d'aujourd'hui*, VIII, Paris 1892; A. Soffici, *P. Cézanne*, Florence 1908, reprinted in *Scoperte e massacri*, Florence 1919; J. Rivière, *Cézanne*, Paris 1910; E. Faure, *P. Cézanne*, Paris 1910; M. Denis,

Théorie, Paris 1912; O. Mirbeau, Th. Duret, J. Werth, F. Jourdain, *Cézanne*, Paris 1914; G. Coquiot, *P. Cézanne*, 1919; C. Carrà, 'P. Cézanne', in *Pittura metafisica*, Florence 1919; G. Rivière, *Le maître P. Cézanne*, Paris 1923; T. Klingsor, *Cézanne*, Paris 1923; A. Salmon, *Cézanne*, Paris 1927; R. Fry, *Cézanne, a study of his development*, London 1927; E. d'Ors, *Cézanne*, Paris 1930; G. Mack, *P. Cézanne*, New York 1935; M. Raynal, *Cézanne*, Paris 1936; J. Rewald, *Cézanne et Zola*, Paris 1936; J. Rewald, *P. Cézanne, sa vie, son œuvre, son amitié pour Zola*, Paris 1939; L. Venturi, *P. Cézanne, aquarelles*, London 1943; R. M. Rilke, *Lettres sur Cézanne*, Paris 1944; M. Merleau-Ponty, 'Le doute de Cézanne', in *Fontaine*, Paris 1945, No. 47; G. Schildt, *Le comportement psychologique de Cézanne, interprétation de son art et de sa personnalité,* Stockholm 1946; J. Rewald, *The History of Impressionism*, 1946; E. Loran, *Cézanne's composition, analysis of his form with diagrams and photographs of his motifs*, Los Angeles 1947; B. Dorival, *Cézanne*, Paris 1948; A. Lhote, *Cézanne*, Lausanne 1949; F. Jourdain, *Cézanne*, Paris 1950; L. Guerry, *Cézanne et l'expression de l'espace*, Paris 1950; G. Marchiori, 'Cézanne', in *Pittura moderna in Europa*, Venice 1950; J. Rewald, 'P. Cézanne', *Carnets de dessins*, Paris 1951; G. Schmidt, *Aquarelles de P. Cézanne*, Basle 1952; L. Venturi, 'Cézanne', in *Enciclopedia Universale dell'Arte,* Florence 1958, Vol. III; M. Schapiro, *Cézanne*, New York 1952; Th. Rousseau, *Cézanne*, Paris 1954; H. Perruchot, *La vie de Cézanne*, Paris 1956; L. Brion-Guerry, *Cézanne et l'expression de l'espace*, Paris 1966.

ARTICLES

G. Rivière, 'L'exposition des impressionnistes', in *L'Impressionniste*, Paris 14 April 1877; J. K. Huysmans, 'Trois peintres, Cézanne, Tisson, Wagner', in *La Cravache*, Paris 4 August 1888 (reprinted in *Certains*, Paris 1889); G. Geffroy, 'P. Cézanne', in *Le Journal*, Paris 25 March 1894; T. Natanson, 'P. Cézanne', in *Revue Blanche*, Paris 1 December 1895; A. Fontaines, 'P. Cézanne', in *Mercure de France*, Paris June 1898; F. Fagus, 'Quarante tableaux de Cézanne', in *Revue Blanche*, Paris 15 December 1899; G.

Lecomte, ' P. Cézanne ', in *Revue d'Art*, Paris 9 December 1899; E. Bernard, ' P. Cézanne ', in *L'Occident*, Paris July 1904; M. Denis, ' Cézanne ', in *L'Ermitage*, Paris 15 November 1905; Ch. Morice, ' Cézanne ' in *Mercure de France*, Paris 15 February 1907; R. Rivière and J. F. Schnerb, ' L'atelier de Cézanne ', in *La Grande Revue*, Paris 25 December 1907; A. Alexandre, ' L'Œuvre de Cézanne ', in *Comoedia*, 15 January 1910; M. Denis, ' Cézanne ', in *Burlington Magazine*, London, January-February 1911; E. Faure, ' P. Cézanne ', in *L'Art Décoratif*, Paris 5 October 1911; A. Gleizes, ' La tradition et le cubisme ', in *Montjoie!*, Paris February 1913; E. Bernard, ' La méthode de P. Cézanne ', in *Mercure de France*, Paris 1920; A. Lhote, ' L'enseignement de Cézanne ', in *N.R.F.*, Paris November 1920; G. Severini, ' Cézanne et le cézannisme ', in *Esprit Nouveau*, Paris November-December 1921; M. J. Friedländer, ' Über P. Cézanne ', in *Die Kunst*, February 1922; M. Denis, ' Le dessin de Cézanne ', in *L'Amour de l'Art*, Paris February 1924; G. Rivière, ' La Formation de Cézanne ', in *L'Amour de l'Art*, 1 August 1925; R. Fry, ' Le développement de Cézanne ' in *L'Amour de l'Art*, December 1926; L. Venturi, ' Sur les dernières années de Cézanne ', in *Minotaure*, Paris 1936, No. 9; J. Rewald, ' A propos du catalogue raisonné de l'œuvre de Cézanne et de la chronologie de cette œuvre ', in *La Renaissance*, Paris March-April 1937; G. Bazin, ' Cézanne et la Montagne Sainte-Victoire ', in *L'Amour de l'Art*, Paris June 1938; J. Rewald, ' P. Cézanne, new documents on the years 1870-1871 ', in *Burlington Magazine*, London April 1939; K. Badt, ' Cézanne and his technique ' in *Burlington Magazine*, London October 1943; J. Bouchot-Saupique, ' Un carnet de croquis de Cézanne ', *La Revue des Arts*, Paris 1951. A thorough study, containing a vast amount of material in the form of articles and notes and edited by J. Lethève, is *Impressionnistes et Symbolistes devant la Presse*, Paris 1959.

Notes on the plates

1 Sorrow (or The Magdalen), 1864-8. Oil on canvas, 165×124 cm. Paris, Louvre. A typical romantic painting. It was originally part of a larger composition, *Christ in Limbo,* taken from an engraving by Charles Blanc, who in his turn was inspired by a work in the Prado attributed to Sebastiano del Piombo. It is the right-hand section.

2-3 The Robbers and the Ass, 1869-70. Oil on canvas, 41×55 cm. Milan, Grassi Collection, in the Galleria d'Arte Moderna. The subject is taken from Apuleius, but Cézanne was probably inspired to paint this work by the picture with the same title by Daumier: the general colour tones and the way of treating the figures have more than one point in common with Daumier's painting. Decamps too had previously painted the same subject.

4 Portrait of Achille Emperaire, 1867-8. Oil on canvas, 200×122 cm. Signed at bottom right. Paris, private collection. Cézanne's friend, the painter Emperaire, is depicted here in dramatic form. Among Cézanne's experiments in romantic painting, this work is already a sound achievement.

5 The Negro Scipion, 1868. Oil on canvas, 107×83 cm. São Paulo (Brazil), Museu de Arte. This is perhaps the most important of the paintings of the romantic period. Cézanne's emotionalism is restrained here and subordinated to the objective depiction of character. The sitter is a popular model from the Académie Suisse. The influence of Ribera may be seen in this work.

6-7 Mont Sainte-Victoire, 1870. Oil on canvas, 80×129 cm. Munich, Bayerische Staatsgemäldesammlungen. A severe and broadly-conceived landscape representing a place near the Jas de Bouffan. A sketch made from the identical viewpoint is in existence. There are indications in this work of the course Cézanne's future development would take: no longer in the romantic tradition, but moving towards realism, and hence impressionism.

8 The Black Clock, 1869-71. Oil on canvas, 54×73 cm. Stavros Niarchos Coll. This still-life foreshadows the values which were later to become fundamental in the art of Cézanne: a restrained and structural method of composition, together with a concrete solidity which imparts a kind of solemnity to the most everyday objects.

9 Black and white still-life, 1871-2. Oil on canvas, 63×80 cm. Paris, Jeu de Paume. Much the same as was said of *pl. 8* applies here. This work still shows an emphasis on contrast between the whites and the blacks, attenuated with touches of lead grey and a yellowish grey, 'studio colours' which have not become suffused with impressionist light.

10-11 Still-life with a medallion by Solari, 1870-2. Oil on canvas, 10×10 cm. Paris, private collection. Another title for this work is *The Accessories of Cézanne.* Philippe Solari was a friend of Cézanne, a sculptor who made a bust of Cézanne in 1904. The medallion is a portrait of Dr Gachet.

12 Portrait of Madame Cézanne, 1872-7. Oil on canvas, 55×46 cm. Pittsburgh, Thompson Collection. Cézanne painted more than forty portraits of his wife, among them some of his greatest masterpieces. This is one of the earliest, and is especially noteworthy for the firm modelling of the face.

13 The Suicide's House, 1872-3. Oil on canvas, 55.5×66.5 cm. Signed at bottom left. Paris, Jeu de Paume. This is considered Cézanne's first impressionist masterpiece. It was painted at Auvers, the home of Dr Gachet. Not far away, at Pontoise, lived Pissarro, whose influence clearly appears in this painting, both in colour and in composition. But the spirit, the energy and feeling for structure were all Cézanne's own. His colour was now becoming very much freer and was already 'colour-light'. And there is a hint of what Cézanne's brushstroke was to become: flat, transparent, yet solid.

14-15 A modern Olympia, 1872-3. Oil on canvas, 46×55 cm. Paris, Jeu de Paume. Another version of this subject was painted in 1870. Why did Cézanne adopt the theme of Manet's famous masterpiece, which had been executed ten years earlier? It was probably with an ironic intention, not towards Manet, but towards the romanticism which had held Cézanne in thrall for some years. The man in front of Olympia is Cézanne himself. The manner of painting is romantic, so that the irony emerges from the essential form of the painting. We may, in fact, consider this work a kind of 'caprice'.

16 The house of Dr Gachet at Auvers, 1873. Oil on canvas, 56×46 cm. Private collection. This painting is mentioned in one of Van Gogh's letters: he saw it at the shop of Le Père Tanguy, the dealer in impressionist and neo-impressionist paintings. It was here that Vollard first discovered the Master of Aix.

17 Auvers, panoramic view, 1873-5. Oil on canvas, 65×81 cm. Chicago, Art Institute. Auvers was a favourite place for the impressionists to go and paint. The landscape is colourful both in spring and summer, and has wide and open views. In this painting Cézanne stands back from the immediate view in order to represent the broad and airy quality of the landscape. More than the preceding works, this seems to follow the impressionist theories very closely: it is more sensitive in touch, more vibrant in colour, fresher in execution. Yet, here again, the distinguishing mark of Cézanne is clearly present: in the structural effect of the well-defined roofs, bringing a decisive firmness to the looser texture of the landscape — the firmness, in fact, which we associate with Cézanne.

18 Dahlias in a Delft vase, 1873-5. Oil on canvas, 73×54 cm. Signed at bottom left. Paris, Jeu de Paume. This was painted at Dr Gachet's house, where Pissarro painted a similar work.

19 Cup and milk jug, 1873-7 Oil on canvas, 20.5×18.5 cm. Tokyo, Ishibashi Collection. This is a splendid still-life, in which Cézanne's concern to give objects a geometric solidity can clearly be seen. In this Cézanne soon reached perfection, and his paint too became less heavy, especially in the landscapes; it tended to remain thicker in the still-lifes.

20 The Jas de Bouffan, 1875-6. Oil on canvas, 46×55 cm. Zurich, private collection. A lively and sensitive study of a view of the property bought by Cézanne's father in 1859.

21 Self-portrait, 1875-7. Oil on canvas, 55×47 cm. Munich, Bayerische Staatsgemäldesammlungen. During his lifetime Cézanne painted thirty or more self-portraits, usually half or three-quarter length. At this date he was a little over thirty-seven years of age.

22-3 Provençal landscape, 1875-8. Watercolour, 37.5×49.5 cm. Zurich, Kunsthaus. Cézanne was a great watercolourist. This rapid technique enabled him to show the essential features of a landscape in a few rapid touches. Between one colour and the next, the whiteness of the page is used to enhance the structural effect.

24-5 Still-life with apples, 1877-8. Oil on canvas, 38×55 cm. Signed at bottom right. Paris, Musée de l'Orangerie. The setting out of the objects required for a still-life was a slow and well-considered process for Cézanne even when, as in this case, the fruit and dish with biscuits appear to have been arranged without any kind of order. The fact is that Cézanne's was not the order which followed the canons of traditional composition. His still-lifes were arranged in the kind of order which avoided a 'manufactured' appearance, while maintaining a rigorous sculptural quality, as in this canvas, where the narrow horizontal plane, on which the fruit bears down in a brilliantly conceived counterpoint of colour, gives unity to the work. It took Cézanne an excessive amount of time to complete a painting, so that in the meantime the fruit used to go bad. He was forced to have recourse to artificial fruit, which would never change colour in the course of his work. Nonetheless, his still-lifes always have the authentic quality of natural objects, although of an unusual firmness and solidity.

26-7 Mountains in Provence, 1878-80. Oil on canvas, 54×73 cm. Cardiff, National Museum of Wales.

28 Château de Médan, 1880. Watercolour, 31×46 cm. Zurich, Kunsthaus. This work was painted at the beginning of Cézanne's period of constructivism. The breakaway from pure impressionism was now complete. He made an oil painting from this watercolour, taking the same viewpoint. Although painted at the same time as the watercolour, the oil reveals a growing tendency to make the form geometrical and proceed by masses. It was probably painted during the summer he spent at Médan as a guest of Zola.

29 Woman with a fan, 1879-82. Oil on canvas, 81×65 cm. Zurich, E. G. Bührle Foundation. This is another portrait of Madame Cézanne. One often has the impression, on looking at a portrait by Cézanne, that there is a lack of emotion and expression of individuality in the sitter. From more than one point of view this impression is justified. Cézanne's portraits never have the immediacy or the psychological emphasis which are characteristic of the other impressionists. Nor have they that weight of emotion which pours from Van Gogh's portraits. This is not what interested Cézanne: he preferred to show what is constant in a character, the 'immutable truth' and primary substance of his personality.

30-1 Still-life, 1879-82. Oil on canvas, 28×34 cm. Emery Reves Collection. The cup and jug are the same as in the still-life in *pl. 19.* There is also a decanter. Although the date given by Venturi, 1873-7, would place this a few years earlier, the two works were probably painted within a short time of each other.

32 Poplars, 1879-82. Oil on canvas, 62×78 cm. Paris, Jeu de Paume. This is an oil painting which has all the spontaneity of a sketch. It should be observed that Cézanne's development, from true impressionism to constructivism, and from constructivism to the synthetic period, did not follow a rectilinear pattern of constant progression. Its course was far more complex and varied, more in the direction of a spiral than of a straight line. This may be seen from the present work.

33 Madame Cézanne in a garden, 1879-82. Oil on canvas, 81×65 cm. Paris, Musée de l'Orangerie. This was painted at the same period as *pls 26-7.* The background is left partly unpainted, which places it in the category of the studies.

34 Farmyard at Auvers, 1879-82. Oil on canvas, 63×52 cm. Paris, Jeu de Paume. This is one of the finest examples of Cézanne's 'constructivist' period.

35 Self-portrait, 1880-1. Oil on canvas, 10×10 cm. Paris, Jeu de Paume. This painting belonged to Pissarro and then to the writer Octave Mirbeau. It has the vigour of a sketch, begun with great enthusiasm, then left unfinished.

36 Two Bathers, 1879-82. Oil on canvas, 40×32 cm. Rome, Marlborough Gallery. A painting of great beauty, which clearly shows Cézanne's method of treating the human anatomy according to sculptural rather than naturalistic criteria.

37 Auvers-sur-Oise seen from Val Harné, 1879-82. Oil on canvas, 73×92 cm. Zurich, private collection.

38-9 Twisted tree, 1882-5. Oil on canvas, 46×55 cm. A. Stoll Collection.

40 The Bridge at Mainey, 1882-5. Oil on canvas, 60×73 cm. Paris, Jeu de Paume. This work also has the title: *The Little Bridge*. It is an admirable example of Cézanne's 'constructivism'. The ideal Cézanne set before himself, to paint nature in its truth, is here fully realized. Nothing remains of his romantic vision of nature but the essence of the natural theme stated in all its objective beauty.

41 Marseilles Bay seen from L'Estaque, 1883-5. Oil on canvas, 58×72 cm. Paris, Louvre. This is a subject dear to Cézanne. Another work with the same title and painted at about the same time is in the Metropolitan Museum of Art in New York. An equally beautiful painting of the same view is in the Art Institute of Chicago. Cézanne liked to paint landscapes from above: he thus gained a broad view, and would circumscribe and block in the landscape with a sure hand. This Mediterranean scene is at one and the same time simple and majestic, human and primordial. The sea appears to rise up vertically as far as the distant mountains.

42-3 Still-life, 1883-7. Oil on canvas, 73×87 cm. Munich, Bayerische Staatsgemäldesammlungen.

44 The Blue Vase, 1883-7. Oil on canvas, 61×50 cm. Paris, Jeu de Paume. This is one of the most perfect flower paintings of Cézanne. The work is pervaded by a diffused blue, yet at the same time the colours are fresh and lively. But the painting is most interesting from the point of view of the structure: the composition is clear-cut, with the horizontal plane of the table, the two wings on the sides (the window and patch of blue on the left) and the diagonal of the settee, which introduces an 'anomaly' between horizontals and perpendiculars. These 'anomalies' were very much liked by Cézanne and added a strange note to the picture, as if there were an invisible inquietude lurking behind the static geometric forms.

45 The Five Bathers, 1885-7. Oil on canvas, 65×65 cm. Basle, Kunsthaus. The subject of bathers is a constantly recurring theme in Cézanne's art. Its presence was especially marked from 1875-7, from 1878-82, from 1883-7, from 1890-4, and finally from 1898 until his death. The theme is fundamentally a classical one, but it is given a new note of naturalism, a happy innocence, through the rhythm of the bodies and the clear light shining among the greenery.

46 Madame Cézanne, 1885-90. Oil on canvas, 81×65 cm. Paris, Musée de l'Orangerie.

47 Houses on the banks of the Marne, 1888-9. Oil on canvas, 65×81 cm. Washington, United States Government.

48-9 Kitchen table, 1888-90. Oil on canvas, 65×81 cm. Paris, Louvre. Also known as *Table with Bread Basket*.

50-1 The Card Players, 1890-2. Oil on canvas, 45×57 cm. Paris, Jeu de Paume. Cézanne painted five versions of this subject. Those with four or five card players are probably of earlier date than the versions with only two; at least that is Venturi's opinion. They were all painted at Aix between 1890 and 1892. This was the culmination of the synthetic period and from this point of view, the version in the Jeu de Paume is certainly the farthest advanced. All these paintings contain something which recalls Courbet's *Afternoon at Ornans*: they have the same strength and rustic vigour, the same simplicity and grandeur. Of course, Cézanne brought everything within the ambit of his own ideal. If we may say that his intention of capturing the 'heroism of the real' can have a special application to any one group of works, there is no doubt that this group would be the five versions of *The Card Players*. Yet although their structure is powerfully represented in its absolute essential aspect, these works, and especially this one in the Jeu de Paume, have a richness of pictorial texture, a delicacy and variety of tone and of light and shade, which is really extraordinary. Here Cézanne's technique reaches its highest point of intensity. This is 'pure' painting, not in the sense of pure form, without human content, but of a human presence identified with form, and free from any virtuosity or external commentary. It is pure in the sense that its style is wholly true, not an artistic exercise.

52 Woman with coffee pot, 1890-4. Oil on canvas, 130×97 cm. Paris, private collection. Cézanne's son dates this work 1887, but Venturi ascribes it to the same period as *The Card Players*; it is certainly close to these paintings in the simplicity of its style.

53 Man with a pipe, 1890-4. Oil on canvas, 73×60 cm. London, Courtauld Institute of Art. This work is part of the same cycle as *The Card Players*. Cézanne did several drawings and paintings of this type of person; he was attracted by their calm, their ancient wisdom, the almost ritualistic world of their gestures.

54 Madame Cézanne in a red dress, 1890-4. Oil on canvas, 91×70 cm. São Paulo (Brazil), Museu de Arte. This, perhaps the purest of all the portraits of his wife which Cézanne painted at about this time, seems to be suspended in the deep red dress, against the pale green background. The unnatural inclination of the body towards the left – another of Cézanne's 'anomalies' – gives the portrait an intimacy and sense of mystery, and within its static form there is a slight sense of loss of balance.

55 Cézanne in a soft hat, 1890-4. Oil on canvas. Tokyo, Ishibashi Collection. This is one of the most spontaneous of his self-portraits.

56-7 The house at Bellevue, 1890-4. Oil on canvas, 60×73 cm. Geneva, private collection. This work may be considered a counterpart to *The Card Players* in the sphere of landscape.

58 Boy in a red waistcoat, 1890-5. Oil on canvas, 79.5×64 cm. Zurich, Bührle Foundation. This is one of a group of portraits in which the same sitter appears, in melancholy and thoughtful mood. The range of colours is more complex than usual.

59 Forest, 1892-4. Oil on canvas. Washington, United States Goverment.

60-1 Rocks in a wood, 1894-8. Oil on canvas, 48.5×59.5 cm. Zurich, Kunsthaus. Cézanne was always particularly interested in painting rocks, but it was about this time that his paintings of rocky landscapes assumed a singular beauty and significance. Among these is the painting *Rocks at Fontainebleau,* now at the Metropolitan Museum of Art, New York. The painting illustrated here is no less fine. Perhaps it was the feeling of a primordial nature contained in the rocks, perhaps their compact, solid and bare form, which so greatly interested Cézanne. Whatever the cause, this subject fitted ideally into Cézanne's vision of painting. For Cézanne these were years of solitude, and this solitude seemed to be reflected in the deserted rocky landscape.

62-3 Still-life with apples and oranges, 1895-1900. Oil on canvas, 54×73 cm. Paris, Jeu de Paume. In these five years Cézanne produced a splendid series of still-lifes, of which this is perhaps the richest in texture and colour. It seems to have been painted in one of his rare moments of happiness.

64 Still-life with onions and bottle, 1895-1900. Oil on canvas, 66×81 cm. Paris, Jeu de Paume. This is another still-life, one of the same series as *pls 62-3.* However, it is less richly coloured, and more rustic. Note the rim of the glass, which opens vertically — a foreshadowing of the cubists.

65 Man with crossed arms, 1895-1900. Oil on canvas, 92×73 cm. New York, Guggenheim Museum.

66 Portrait of Ambroise Vollard, 1899. Oil on canvas, 100×81 cm. Paris, Petit Palais. Besides being painted by Cézanne, Vollard was also the subject of portraits by Bonnard, Maurice Denis, Renoir, Picasso, Rouault and Dufy. He was a great dealer, a man of vision, and organized many exhibitions. It was he who organized Cézanne's first large exhibition in 1895. He was also responsible for arranging the first French exhibition of Picasso's work in 1900, and of Matisse in 1904.

67 Park at Château Noir, 1900. Oil on canvas, 73×60 cm.

68-9 The Great Bathers, 1900-5. Oil on canvas, 130×95 cm. Paris, private collection. The return to this theme towards the end of his life corresponds in Cézanne to a renewal of that youthful enthusiasm which had inspired his first romantic period. Of course, none of his stylistic and expressive achievements, gathered in the course of his long experience, was rejected here. It is here that his first romantic aspirations, his search for a form of classicism, his impressionistic feeling for nature, find their soundest point of fusion.

70-1 The Great Bathers, 1898-1905. Oil on canvas, 208×249 cm. Philadelphia, Museum of Art. This is the painting in the series in which Cézanne was most deeply involved, and also the largest canvas he ever painted. It is said to have taken more than seven years to paint. The brushstrokes are broad, free and limpid. What has been said of the previous work applies here too. What must be added is that in this particular composition, in which Cézanne is seeking an effect of grandeur and monumentality, a concern for an order of composition is more apparent, both in the arrangement of the nudes in two groups and in the triangular structure marked by the trees which meet in the upper central portion of the canvas.

72 The Red Rock, 1900. Oil on canvas, 91×66 cm. Paris, Musée de l'Orangerie. The square rock, orange-red on its right side, the sun of the same colour but with violet shadows, the greenish-blue foliage and bright blue sky, make of this painting something simultaneously solid and ardent.

73 Country road, 1900-6. Oil on canvas, 81×65 cm. Munich, Bayerische Staatsgemäldesammlungen.

74-5 Mont Sainte-Victoire, 1904-6. Oil on canvas, 73×92 cm. Philadelphia, Museum of Art. This is the last of Cézanne's great themes. What has been said of Cézanne's return to lyricism in *The Great Bathers* applies also to this series of paintings. In the course of his career, Cézanne depicted Mont Sainte-Victoire at least sixty-five times, in sketches, drawings and oils.

76-7 Mont Sainte-Victoire, 1904-6. Oil on canvas, 65×81 cm. Zurich, Kunsthaus. A rapidly executed work, with broad, square brushstrokes. It is almost a sketch, vibrant with light yet firm.

78-9 Mont Sainte-Victoire, 1904-6. Oil on canvas, 60×73 cm. Basle, Kunsthaus. This is perhaps the most 'enraptured' of the representations of Cézanne's mountain: a profound and total rapture, yet expressed without mysticism and without losing sight of the objective beauty of the world.

1

5

4

7

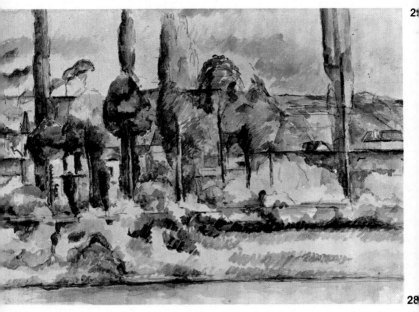

34

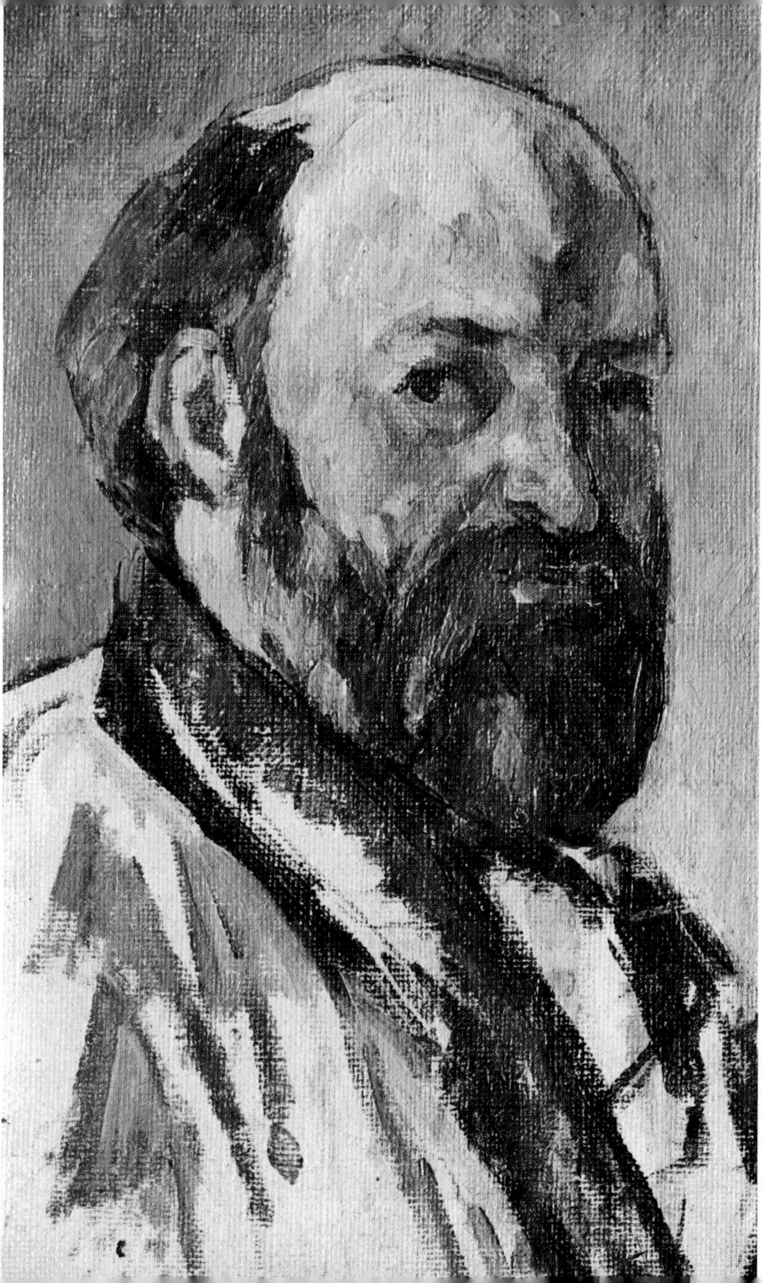

35

39

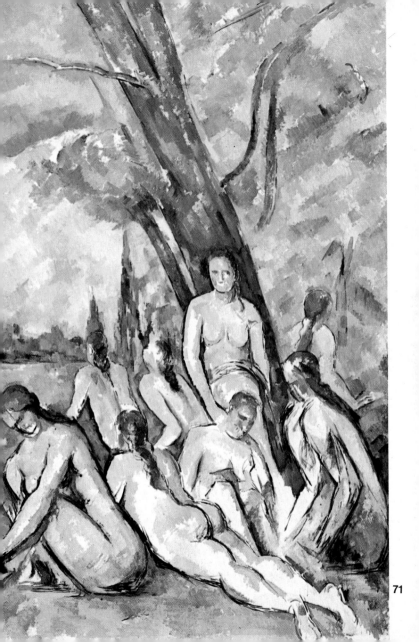

71